First Steps in Academic Writing

SECOND EDITION

Answer Key

Ann Hogue

PEARSON
Longman

First Steps in Academic Writing, Second Edition
Answer Key

Pearson Education, 10 Bank Street, White Plains, NY 10606

Staff credits: The people who made up the *First Steps in Academic Writing Answer Key* team, representing
editorial, production, design, and manufacturing, are: Wendy Campbell, Laura Le Dréan, Edith Pullman,
Robert Ruvo, and Barbara Sabella.

Text composition: Integra
Text font: Times 11.5/14.5

LONGMAN ON THE WEB

Longman.com offers online resources for
teachers and students. Access our Companion
Websites, our online catalog, and our local
offices around the world.

Visit us at **longman.com**.

ISBN 10: 0-13-241490-2
ISBN 13: 978-0-13-241490-6

Printed in the United States of America
6 7 8 9 10—OPM—11 10 09

Contents

Chapter 1: Introducing People

Practice 1: Editing Paragraph Form (pages 8–9)

Amy Wong
[Name of class]
[Month day, 20___]

<u>My Classmate</u>

     My classmate is a very nice person. Her name is

Phuong Pham. She is from Vietnam. In Vietnam she

was a pharmacist. She is married. She lives with her

husband, her children, and her parents-in-law in a

house. Phuong is taking an art class, two English classes,

computer science, and math. She likes to listen to music

and to read books. She doesn't have a job right now but

plans to get one when she finishes school.

Practice 2: Recognizing Sentences (page 12)

A. Sentences 6 and 10 are commands.

B.   3. NS. The verb is missing.
     4. S
     5. NS. The subject is missing.
     6. S
     7. S
     8. NS. The subject is missing.
     9. S
    10. NS. The verb is missing.
    11. NS. The verb *like* requires an object (*the new teacher, the class, the game, it*, etc.).
    12. NS. The verb *want* requires an object (*a test, homework, a test, it, them*, etc.).
    13. S

Practice 3: Subjects, Verbs, and Objects (pages 14–15)

3. He works at a shopping mall.

4. He likes (his job) but doesn't like (his boss).

5. His job is easy and pays well.

6. This semester, he is taking (extra classes).

7. He will go to college next year.

8. He speaks and understands (English) very well.

9. On weekends, he and his friends play (soccer).

10. He doesn't have a (girlfriend) yet.

Practice 4: Editing for Subjects and Verbs (page 15)

Answers will vary. Sample responses:

3. **He** arrives ten minutes late everywhere.
4. Larry always **has/gives** an excuse.
12. Larry's bad habit **is** not a problem for me any longer.
13. If the movie **begins/starts/is** at 7:00, I tell Larry 6:45.
14. Then he **is/arrives/comes** early!

Practice 5: Identifying and Punctuating Sentences (page 15)

A young couple from India lives next door to me. The husband's name is Ajay. The wife's name is Anjuli. Everyone calls her Anju. They have a young son and are expecting their second child in a few weeks. They hope to have a girl this time. Both Ajay and Anju have good jobs. He is an executive in a computer company. She is a computer programmer and works in our local hospital. Anju is a wonderful cook. She cooks mostly Indian food. They sometimes invite neighbors on weekends for a potluck meal. We all bring something to share. It is fun to live next door to Ajay and Anju.

Practice 6: Capitalization (page 17)

Individual responses.

Practice 7: Editing for Capitalization (page 18)

[1]My name is Nelson Mandela, and I have had an unusual life. [2]I have been both a prisoner and a president in my country. [3]I was born in 1918 in a small village in South

Africa. **⁴My father, Henry Mandela,** was the chief of our tribe. **⁵As a child, I** took care of the family's cattle and goats. **⁶When I grew up, I** decided to become a lawyer. **⁷This** seemed to be a good way to help my people. **⁸After I became a lawyer, I** became the leader of a group of young **Africans** who wanted to change the system of discrimination in our country. **⁹Because of my political activities, I** went to prison for twenty-seven years. **¹⁰The prison** was on a cold, windy island in the **Atlantic Ocean.** **¹¹However,** the world didn't forget about me. **¹²I** received important visitors, awards, and university degrees from all over the world. **¹³I** also learned **Afrikaans,** which is the language of white **South Africans.** **¹⁴Of course, I** also speak **English** and **Xhosa,** which is the language of my tribe. **¹⁵In 1990, I** was set free. **¹⁶I** became the president of **South Africa** in 1994. **¹⁷During my time in office, I** tried to bring peace, democracy, and prosperity to all of my country's people. **¹⁸Now I** am retired.

Practice 8: Simple Sentence Patterns (pages 21–22)

A.

2. Every day, <u>he</u> [S] <u>swims</u> [V] a mile and <u>works</u> [V] in his garden.

3. <u>He</u> [S] and <u>my grandmother</u> [S] <u>have</u> [V] four children and ten grandchildren.

4. <u>My grandfather</u> [S] <u>loves</u> [V] parties and <u>invites</u> [V] our entire family to his house for a big dinner on his birthday.

5. <u>All twenty</u> [S] of us <u>eat</u> [V] and <u>tell</u> [V] stories half the night.

6. <u>He</u> [S] never <u>gets</u> [V] tired and <u>is</u> [V] always the last to go to bed.

7. On his last birthday, <u>my brothers</u> [S] and <u>I</u> [S] <u>gave</u> [V] him a present.

8. <u>We</u> [S] <u>put</u> [V] our money together and <u>bought</u> [V] him a video game system.

9. Now <u>he</u> [S] <u>invites</u> [V] us to his house every weekend to play video games with him.

10. <u>My grandfather</u> [S] <u>will</u> always <u>seem</u> [V] young to me.

2. SVV	5. SVV	8. SVV
3. SSV	6. SVV	9. SV
4. SVV	7. SSV	10. SV

B. Answers may vary.

Practice 9: Using *and, or* (page 24)
2. I can speak and understand English.
3. I can't speak Tagalog or Vietnamese.
4. Blue and yellow are my favorite colors.
5. Would you like soup or salad?
6. You can eat your pizza here or take it home.
7. Helen Keller, a famous American woman, was blind and deaf.
8. She could not see or hear.
9. With the help of her teacher, Helen learned to speak and became a famous spokesperson for handicapped people all over the world.

Try It Out! (pages 26–27)

¹I am a famous cartoon animal. ²I have big black ears. ³I always wear red shorts and white gloves. ⁴I look like an animal and (but) talk like a human. ⁵I live and work in a place called Disneyland. ⁶In Disneyland, ⁷I stand around and smile a lot. ⁸I usually team up with my friend Goofy or my friend Minnie. ⁹Together we greet visitors and pose for photographs. ¹⁰I am Mickey Mouse.

Review Questions (pages 27–28)
1. A paragraph is a group of related sentences about a single topic.
2. No, it cannot. The topic of a paragraph is one, and only one, idea.
3. The three parts of a paragraph are the topic sentence, supporting sentences, and the concluding sentence.
4. You write the title in the center above the paragraph.
5. Indenting means starting the first sentence of a paragraph to the right about $\frac{1}{2}$ inch or 5 spaces on a computer.
6. Margins are empty spaces on the left, right, top, and bottom edges of a page.
7. A sentence is a group of words that contains a subject and a verb and expresses a complete thought. A sentence begins with a capital letter and ends with a period.
8. A subject tells who or what did something. It is a noun or pronoun. A verb usually tells an action. Sometimes it just links the subject with the rest of the sentence.
9. Yes, sentences in English always have a subject. The only exception is command sentences. A command sentence does not have a subject.
10. Yes, sentences in English always have a verb. There are no exceptions to this rule.
11. No, sentences in English do not always have an object.
12. See page 16 in the text.
13. A simple sentence is a sentence that has one subject-verb pair.
14. SV; SSV; SVV; SSVV
15. Use *and* to connect two or more items in a positive sentence.
16. a. Use *or* to connect two or more items in a negative sentence.
    b. Use *or* to connect choices.

Chapter 2: Listing-Order Paragraphs

Questions on the Model (page 37)
1. The topic is *flight attendants*.
2. It says they have three important characteristics.
3. Three.
4. Flight attendants are (1) friendly, (2) self-confident, and (3) strong.
5. It repeats the three points.

Practice 1: Two Parts of a Topic Sentence (pages 39–40)
Paragraph 2
(Beaches) are fun in summer and in winter.
Paragraph 3
(Beaches) differ in various parts of the world.
Paragraph 4
People of all ages have fun at (beaches).

Practice 2: Topic Sentences (pages 41–43)
A. 2. (College students) take many kinds of tests.
   3. (Small cars) have several advantages.
   4. (Big cars) are safer than small cars for two reasons.
   5. (A baseball player) must master several skills.
   6. (Living with your parents) has certain advantages.
   7. (Living with your parents) has certain disadvantages.
   8. Talent and dedication are (two characteristics of Olympic athletes.)
   9. (The Middle East) is the birthplace of three major religions.
   10. (Tokyo) has excellent public transportation systems.
   11. (Tokyo) is one of the world's most expensive cities.

B. 1. c   3. b
   2. a   4. c

C. Answers will vary. Sample responses:
   1. There are three kinds of Thai curry.
   2. Good teachers have three main characteristics.
   3. There are three kinds of shoppers.

D. Answers will vary. Sample responses:
   2. International students study English for many different reasons.
      International students are used to different teaching methods.
   3. Hollywood is no longer the center of the movie-making business.
      Many Hollywood movies have amazing special effects.
   4. There are four kinds of dangerous automobile drivers on the roads today.
      Automobile drivers have different driving styles in different countries.
   5. My city has an amazing variety of restaurants.
      My ideal restaurant has the following characteristics.
   6. Bangkok has many tourist attractions.
      Driving a car in Bangkok presents many interesting challenges.

Practice 3: Supporting Sentences (pages 44–45)

Answers will vary. Sample responses:

2. a. placement tests
   b. midterm tests
   c. final exams

3. a. easier to park
   b. less expensive to operate
   c. cheaper to buy

4. a. more engine power
   b. stronger body

5. a. batting
   b. running
   c. throwing
   d. catching

6. a. Rent and food are free.
   b. Mother does laundry and cleans room.
   c. Parents are available to give advice.

7. a. My parents want to know where I am every minute.
   b. I have to call them when I want to stay out late.
   c. I have no privacy.

Practice 4: Listing-Order Transition Signals (page 46)

A. Signals for three main points: *First of all, Second, Third*
   Other listing-order signal in the paragraph: *also*

B. Answers may vary. Sample responses:
   1. First of all,   2. Second,   3. also   4. In addition,   5. (,) also (with or without a comma)

Practice 5: Paragraph Unity (page 47)

Paragraph 1:
   Topic Sentence: (California) is a state with every kind of geography.
   Cross out sentences 7 and 8.

Paragraph 2:
   Topic Sentence: (A nurse) should have at least five characteristics.
   Cross out sentences 8 and 11.

Practice 6: Concluding Sentences (pages 49–51)

A. Paragraph 1:   c

   Paragraph 2:   a

B. Answers will vary. Sample responses:

1. In conclusion, to have a quiet, economical, and trouble-free pet, visit your nearest goldfish store.
2. In conclusion, Singapore has it all. (OR) For a safe, clean, peaceful city with a high standard of living, consider Singapore.

C. Answers will vary depending on students' answers in Practice 3. Sample responses:

2. In short, students take tests before, during, and at the end of every term.
3. In short, for easy parking, low operating costs, and affordable price, my next car is going to be a small car.
4. In summary, big cars have more power and stronger bodies, so they will keep you and your family safe in most driving situations.
5. In brief, the four basic skills of baseball are batting, running, throwing, and catching.
6. In conclusion, free rent, free food, free laundry and maid service, and free advice is a very good deal.
7. In conclusion, loss of freedom, independence, and privacy are some of the disadvantages of living at home.

Practice 7: Outlining (page 52)

Individual outlines.

Practice 8: Simple versus Compound Sentences (pages 54–56)

A.

simple	svv	3. <u>Our parents</u> <u>sat</u> in chairs on the grass and <u>watched</u> us play our children's games.
compound	sv, *or* svv	4. <u>We</u> <u>played</u> games such as hide-and-seek and tag, (or) <u>we</u> just <u>sat</u> on the grass and <u>told</u> stories.
simple	sv	5. <u>We</u> also <u>caught</u> fireflies.
compound	sv, *and* sv	6. <u>We</u> <u>put</u> the fireflies into glass jars, (and) <u>our father</u> <u>punched</u> air holes in the metal lid.
compound	sv, *but* sv	7. <u>My sisters</u> <u>were</u> afraid of most bugs, (but) <u>they</u> <u>loved</u> fireflies.
compound	sv, *but* sv	8. <u>We</u> usually <u>went</u> to bed at nine o'clock, (but) <u>we</u> <u>stayed up</u> until ten on really warm evenings.
simple	ssv	9. Around ten o'clock <u>our mother and father</u> <u>told</u> us to come inside.
compound	(s) v, *but* (s) v	10. "<u>Come</u> inside now, (but) <u>leave</u> the fireflies outside, please," our mother always said. (Instruct students to analyze only the part of the sentence inside the quotation marks.)

ESL Department
Utah Valley University

B.

¹<u>Teenagers</u> <u>find</u> many ways to drive their parents crazy. ²First, <u>they</u> <u>dye</u> their hair purple, or <u>they</u> <u>shave</u> their heads bald. ³<u>They</u> also <u>tattoo</u> their skin and <u>wear</u> rings in their noses. ⁴In addition, <u>they</u> <u>spend</u> hours at the shopping mall and on the phone. ⁵<u>They</u> <u>have</u> time to watch TV, but <u>they</u> <u>don't have</u> time to do their homework. ⁶Also, <u>they're</u> always too busy to clean up their rooms, but <u>they're</u> never too busy to clean out the refrigerator by eating everything in it. ⁷Finally, <u>they</u> <u>are</u> old enough to drive but too young to pay for gas. ⁸<u>They</u> <u>are</u> usually broke, so <u>they</u> always <u>return</u> the family car with an empty gas tank. ⁹<u>It's</u> hard to be a teenager, but <u>it's</u> even harder to be the parent of one.

2. compound	sv, *or* sv
3. simple	svv
4. simple	sv
5. compound	sv, *but* sv
6. compound	sv, *but* sv
7. simple	sv
8. compound	sv, *so* sv
9. compound	sv, *but* sv

Practice 9: *And, but, so*, and *or* in Simple and Compound Sentences (page 57)

2. and	6. so	10. so
3. or	7. or, but	11. or, so
4. but	8. so	12. or
5. and, but	9. and	13. but

Practice 10: Writing Compound Sentences (pages 57–59)

A. 2. There are several hundred languages in the world, but not all of them have a written form.

    3. Chinese is spoken by more people, but English is spoken in more countries.

    4. Russian is the third most spoken language in the world, and Spanish is the fourth.

    5. There are about one million words in English, but most people use only about ten thousand of them.

    6. Chinese has many different dialects, so Chinese people cannot always understand each other.

    7. French used to be the language of international diplomacy, but now it is English.

    8. International companies are growing, so/and they will soon need more bilingual workers.

    9. Young people should know a second language, or they will be at a disadvantage in the international job market.

B. Answers will vary. Sample responses:

    2. We are both medium tall, and we have wavy hair.

    3. He is an extrovert, but I am shy.

    4. I am younger, so he was always the boss.

    5. Our mother used to tell us, "Stop fighting, or you can't watch TV for a week."

    6. We fought a lot as children, but now we are good friends.

    7. We married two sisters, so we see each other often.

Practice 11: Fixing Run-Ons and Comma Splices (pages 60–61)

X   2. Kittens are cute. Also, they like to play. (*Also*) Kittens are cute, and they also like to play.

X   4. It's acceptable for dogs to bark at strangers. They shouldn't bite them, however. (*Also*) It's acceptable for dogs to bark at strangers, but they shouldn't bite them.

X   6. Penguins always wear tuxedos. They are good pets for people who like to go to fancy parties. (*Also*) Penguins always wear tuxedos, so they are good pets for people who like to go to fancy parties.

X   7. A pet elephant can fan you with his ears and spray you with his trunk. You won't need air-conditioning or a shower. (*Also*) A pet elephant can fan you with his ears and spray you with his trunk, so you won't need air-conditioning or a shower.

X   9. A giraffe can reach things on high shelves. Also, it can see over the heads of people at parades. (*Also*) A giraffe can reach things on high shelves, and it can see over the heads of people at parades.

X 10. Keep a boa constrictor as a pet if you enjoy being alone. Then no one will ever visit you. (*Also*) Keep a boa constrictor as a pet if you enjoy being alone, and then no one will ever visit you.

Try It Out! (pages 62–63)

Answers will vary. Samples responses:

¹It is often said that women are the weaker sex, but women are actually superior to men in several ways. ²First of all, women live longer and stay healthier than men in all countries of the world. ³This difference starts at birth and continues until old age. ⁴On the average, women live seven years longer than men in the United States. ⁵There are 105 boys to every 100 girls at birth, but there are twice as many women as men at age 80. ⁶Second, women are better than men at things that involve the five senses. ⁷Women have a sharper sense of taste and smell. ⁸Third, men are physically stronger than women, but women are mentally stronger. ⁹For example, more men than women had emotional problems during bombing attacks on London in World War II. ¹⁰Do you still believe that women are "the weaker sex?"

Review Questions (page 63)

1. Clustering is a prewriting technique. You begin by writing your topic in a circle in the center of a piece of paper. Then you write ideas in smaller circles around the topic. The end result is clusters of circles.

2. Listing order is a pattern of organizing ideas in a paragraph. In listing order, you divide a topic into separate points and discuss each point one after the other.

3. The three parts of a paragraph are the topic sentence, supporting sentences, and the concluding sentence.

4. The two parts of a topic sentence are the topic and the controlling idea.

5. The controlling idea tells the reader what the paragraph will say about the topic.

6. Transition signals are words and phrases that show how one idea is related to another idea. Some listing-order transition signals are *First, Second, Third, Also,* and *In addition.*

7. Unity means that all the sentences in a paragraph are about one main idea.

8. (1) You can restate the topic sentence in different words. (2) You can summarize the main points.

9. An outline is a plan for a paragraph. An outline helps writers by making them organize their ideas before they start writing.

10. The formula for a compound sentence is this: Simple sentence, coordinating conjunction, simple sentence.

11. Put the comma in a compound sentence before the coordinating conjunction.

12. Two common sentence errors are comma splices and run-ons.

13. (1) Make two separate sentences by using a period and a capital letter. (2) Make a compound sentence by adding a coordinating conjunction (and a comma, if there isn't one.)

Chapter 3: Giving Instructions

Questions on the Model (page 68)
1. The topic is garage sales.
2. The first sentence tells you the topic. It is called the topic sentence.
3. The paragraph explains 7 main steps.
4. Transition signals: *First, Next, Third, Fourth, Then, Finally, After that*
5. The paragraph uses time order.

Practice 1: Topic Sentences for "How To" Paragraphs (pages 69–70)
A. Answers will vary. Sample responses:
    2. It is simple to make a Halloween jack-o-lantern if you follow these instructions.
    3. Anyone can learn to turn on snow skis if he or she follows this procedure.
    4. Follow these instructions to bid successfully on eBay.
    5. Write a perfect paragraph by following these steps.
B. Individual responses.

Practice 2: Listing Order or Time Order? (pages 71–72)

3. TO	7. TO
4. LO	8. TO
5. LO	9. TO
6. LO	10. LO

Practice 3: Transition Signals (pages 72–73)
Transition signals added to the paragraphs may vary.
1. How to Prevent Jet Lag (Use time order.)
    __1__ Frequent flyers recommend these steps to prevent jet lag.
    __3__ Don't drink alcohol or coffee during the flight.
    __5__ Go to bed early your first night in the new time zone.
    __2__ Eat a high-carbohydrate meal before your flight.
    __4__ Don't nap during the day when you arrive.

Frequent flyers recommend these steps to prevent jet lag. First of all, eat a high-carbohydrate meal before your flight. Second, don't drink alcohol or coffee during the flight. Third, don't nap during the day when you arrive. Finally, go to bed early your first night in the new time zone.

2. How to Drive Your Teacher Crazy (Use time order.)
    __1__ It's easy to drive your teacher crazy if you follow these simple directions.
    __4__ Yawn and look at your watch as often as possible during the class.
    __3__ Make a lot of noise when you enter the classroom.
    __5__ At least five minutes before the end of class, slam your books shut and stare at the door.
    __2__ Always come to class at least five minutes late.

It's easy to drive your teacher crazy if you follow these simple directions. First, always come to class at least five minutes late. Also, make a lot of noise when you enter the classroom. Then yawn and look at your watch as often as possible during the class. Finally, at least five minutes before the end of class, slam your books shut and stare at the door.

3. How to Plan a Family Vacation (Use listing order. Except for the sentences marked "1" and "6," the sentences can be in any order.)

_____ Consider the interests and abilities of everyone in the family.

_____ Decide how long you can be away from home.

_____ Decide how much money you can spend.

___1___ Planning a family vacation takes careful thought.

_____ Find out when everyone can take time off from school and jobs.

___6___ When you have the answers to all of these questions, visit a travel agency.

Planning a family vacation takes careful thought. First of all, find out when everyone can take time off from school and jobs. Also, decide how long you can be away from home. Third, consider the interests and abilities of everyone in the family. In addition, decide how much money you can spend. When you have the answers to all of these questions, visit a travel agency.

4. How to Wax a Car (Use time order.)

___1___ Keep your car looking great by following these easy steps to wax it.

___6___ After you have put wax on the entire car, start to remove it, section by section.

___3___ Wash and dry the car thoroughly.

___7___ Use a soft towel to remove the wax in the same order that you applied it.

___5___ Work on one section at a time, and rub the wax into the car in small circles.

___2___ Park your car in a cool, shady spot.

___8___ Polish the car with a soft cloth to remove any remaining wax and to bring out the shine.

___4___ Dip a damp sponge into a can of wax.

Keep your car looking great by following these easy steps to wax it. First, park your car in a cool, shady spot. Then wash and dry the car thoroughly. Next, dip a damp sponge into a can of wax. Work on one section at a time, and rub the wax into the car in small circles. After you have put wax on the entire car, start to remove it, section by section. Use a soft towel to remove the wax in the same order that you applied it. Finally, polish the car with a soft cloth to remove any remaining wax and to bring out the shine.

Practice 4: Simple Outlining (page 76)
Individual outlines.

Practice 5: Independent and Dependent Clauses (page 79)

3. IC
4. IC
5. DC – When
6. IC
7. DC – After
8. IC

9. IC
10. DC – When
11. IC
12. DC – as soon as
13. IC

Practice 6: Complex Sentences with Time Subordinators (pages 80–82)

A. 2. We were very excited (when) we won.
    3. (After) we got our first payment, we started planning a trip to Italy.
    4. (Before) we left on our trip, we wrote to our cousins in Rome and told them our plans.
    5. (As soon as) they received our letter, they called and invited us to stay with them.
    6. They were waiting at the airport (when) we arrived.
    7. They waited outside (while) the Italian officials checked our passports and luggage.
    8. Finally, (after) we got our suitcases, they drove us to their home.
    9. (As soon as) we arrived at their apartment, they wanted to feed us.
    10. We ate one delicious home-cooked dish after another (until) we were stuffed.
    11. We fell asleep (as soon as) our heads hit the pillows.
    12. Almost 24 hours had passed (since) we left home.

B. 1. b
    2. g
    3. f
    4. e

    5. h
    6. a
    7. d
    8. c

The trip began badly when we had a flat tire on the way to the lake. It was almost noon before we started fishing. As soon as I threw out my fishing line, it got caught in some underwater weeds. I spent most of the afternoon untangling my line while my brothers were catching fish after fish. After we had been fishing for a couple of hours, it started to rain. We were totally wet before we could put on our rain jackets. When we got back home, I immediately took a hot shower. It will be a long, long time before I go fishing with my brothers again.

C. 1. I take a walk around the block before I go to work.
    2. When I go to work, it is still dark.
    3. After I get home from work, it is dark again.
    4. When it is raining, of course, I never go out.
    5. On rainy days, as soon as the alarm clock rings, I turn over and go back to sleep.

ESL Department
Utah Valley University

Practice 7: Fragments (page 82)

Sentences will vary. Possible sentences:

2. F Every night, after I finish my homework, I watch TV.
3. F We ran outside as soon as we heard the crash.
4. S
5. S
6. F My husband has to take a day off from work whenever our children have a school holiday.
7. S

Practice 8: Simple, Compound, and Complex Sentences (pages 83–84)

A. compound 2. <u>Other people like to travel</u>, and <u>still others like to have an adventure.</u>

    simple 3. <u>Unusual vacations are becoming popular.</u>

    simple 4. <u>For example, people go hiking in Nepal or river rafting in Ecuador.</u>

    compound 5. <u>Some people spend their vacations learning</u>, and <u>some spend their vacations helping others.</u>

    compound 6. <u>A friend of mine likes to help people</u>, so <u>he spent his summer helping to build a school in Bangladesh.</u>

    complex 7. <u>After he returned home</u>, <u>he wanted to go back to help build a medical clinic.</u>

    complex 8. <u>People may find the local scenery a little boring</u> <u>after they have climbed volcanoes in Guatemala or ridden camels in Egypt.</u>

B. 1. Compound sentences: 9, 11, 12, 13, and 16
    2. Complex sentences: 5, 7, and 8

Try It Out! (pages 84–86)

Answers will vary. Sample responses:

[1]Would you like to own a pair of designer jeans but can't afford to pay designer prices? [2]Follow these instructions to make your own pair of stylishly ripped and faded jeans. [3]First, buy a pair of inexpensive new jeans, or use a pair that you already own. [4]Second, find the direction of the lines in the denim fabric, and rub a knife back and forth in the opposite direction. [5]You can also use a cheese grater or a nail file. [6]Keep rubbing until white threads appear. [7]You want the white threads to stay there, so don't cut them. [8]Next, dip an old toothbrush into bleach, and run it around the edges of the back pockets and over the belt loops. [9]After that, mix a little bleach with water in a spray bottle, and spray the thighs and seat of the jeans. [10]Then rub sandpaper on the hems of the legs to fray them, and rip one corner of a back pocket. [11]After you wash and dry the jeans several times, your new jeans will look stylishly old!

Practice 9: Capitalization (pages 87–88)

A. Individual responses.

B.

Dear Stacie,

[1]I am so happy that you are coming to visit me this summer. [2]I hope that you will be able to stay until July 4. [3]We are planning a big picnic on that day to celebrate Independence Day here in the United States.

[4]You asked for directions to my house from the airport, so here they are. [5]Drive out of the airport and turn north on U.S. 380, then U.S. 680, then California 1. [6]California 1 is also called Nineteenth Avenue. [7]You will pass San Francisco State University and a large shopping center.

[8]Continue on Nineteenth Avenue through Golden Gate Park. [9]Soon you will come to the famous Golden Gate Bridge. [10]Drive across the bridge and continue north for about ten more miles. [11]You will pass the towns of Sausalito, Mill Valley, and Larkspur. [12]In Larkspur, take the Sir Francis Drake Boulevard exit from the highway.

[13]Drive west for three blocks, and then turn left. [14]Pacific National Bank is on the corner where you turn, and across the street is a Shell Oil Company gas station. [15]You will be on Elm Avenue. [16]Finally, go one block on Elm and turn right. [17]My apartment is in the Marina Towers. [18]The address is 155 West Hillside Drive.

[19]Be sure to bring warm clothes because it is cold in June and July in northern California. [20]I can't wait to see you!

Love,
Heather

Practice 10: Commas (pages 90–92)

A. Paragraph 1

[1]My brother Bob is a sports fan. [2]His favorite sports are golf, tennis, skiing, and swimming. [3]He skis in the winter, swims in the summer, and plays golf during the spring, summer, and fall. [4]He also watches football and baseball on TV. [5]His bedroom looks like a used sporting goods store. [6]Bob owns skis, tennis racquets, golf clubs, footballs, basketballs, baseballs, tennis balls, soccer balls, a bicycle, and weights. [7]Whenever he comes home from a sports event, he throws his equipment in a pile on his bed. [8]When the pile gets too high, you can't see his bed, his desk, or sometimes even him.

Paragraph 2

[1]It's easy to fail a driving test if you really try. [2]First, park your car so close to the next car that the examiner cannot get into your car to begin the test. [3]It also helps to have your two front wheels far up on the curb—blocking the sidewalk if possible. [4]Second, back out of the parking space really fast. [5]After that, try to hit something such as another car. [6]Don't stop at stop signs, but speed up to get through intersections quickly. [7]Then try to make your tires squeal while turning corners. [8]Next, look for an opportunity to turn the wrong way on a one-way street. [9]Entering a one-way street in the wrong direction will cause you to fail immediately. [10]Finally, don't stop for pedestrians in crosswalks, but use your horn to frighten them out of your way. [11]Just one of these techniques will probably get you an F on a driving test, and two or more certainly will.

15

B. Answers will vary. Sample responses:
  2. I don't like spinach, carrots, or beets.
  3. On my honeymoon, I might go to Tahiti, Australia, or nowhere.
  4. Whenever you go on a hike, be sure to take water, sunglasses, a map, a hat, a jacket, and a whistle.
  5. Cats and mice don't get along with each other.
  6. Every morning I turn off my alarm clock, get out of bed, and practice yoga for an hour.
  7. On weekends, I always sleep late and watch a lot of TV, but I never do homework.

Review Questions (page 92)
  1. The four keys are (1) begin with a topic sentence that names the topic and says the paragraph will give instructions about it, (2) divide the instructions into a series of steps, (3) explain each step one by one, and (4) use a transition signal to introduce each step.
  2. You can use time order or listing order.
  3. Time-order transition signals: *First, Second, Then, Next, After that, Finally.*
  4. An independent clause has one SV combination and expresses a complete thought. *Independent clause* is just another name for a simple sentence.
  5. A dependent clause is an independent clause with a subordinating word, such as *because, after*, and *when*, added to the beginning of it.
  6. A complex sentence is one independent and one dependent clause. If the dependent clause comes first, put a comma after it. If the independent clause comes first, don't use a comma.
  7. A fragment is an incomplete sentence, or part of a sentence.
  8. Add an independent clause.
  9. See page 86 in the text.
  10. See page 89 in the text.

Chapter 4: Describing a Place

Questions on the Model (page 99)
1. Sentence 2.
2. Top to bottom.

Practice 1: Space Order (page 100)
1. Topic: my nephew. Controlling idea: he is extremely tall.
2. His height
3. Sentence 12; tall.
4. Top to bottom.

Practice 2: Being Specific (pages 101–102)
Answers will vary. Sample responses:

2. a. There is an elegant entry hall with lots of mirrors.
   b. There are gardens, a tennis court, and two swimming pools.
   c. The outside of the house is imported stone.
   d. There are Persian carpets everywhere.

3. a. He always drives 20 mph above the speed limit.
   b. He doesn't obey traffic lights.
   c. He changes lanes frequently.
   d. He never uses his turn signals.

4. a. There were greasy stains on the seats.
   b. Candy wrappers and empty cigarette packages littered the floor.
   c. You couldn't see through the windows.
   d. The door handles were sticky.

5. a. Every table was occupied.
   b. The cafeteria line stretched out the door.
   c. Students yelled across the room to their friends.
   d. Dishes, trays, and utensils banged together.

Practice 3: Adding Specific Details (pages 102–103)
Individual responses. Sample paragraph:

The Limousine

The limousine was quite luxurious. It was at least fifteen feet long. It had six doors and could carry ten passengers comfortably. The outside of the limousine was silver in color. The shine from so much chrome hurt your eyes. The inside had soft white leather seats and thick white carpet. There was a sound system, a television set, a VCR, and a shelf full of movies to watch. There was also a refrigerator full of drinks, a bucket of ice, two trays of sandwiches, a large bowl of fruit, and several small bowls of nuts and candy.

ESL Department
Utah Valley University

Practice 4: Space-Order Outline (page 103)

Suggested response:

The Shared Refrigerator

> My roommate's half of our refrigerator is very neat.

> A. On the top shelf is a carton of milk, a pitcher of orange juice, and a bottle of mineral water.
>
> B. On the next shelf are cans of soda.
>
> C. On the third shelf, he keeps dairy food, such as butter, cheese, eggs, and yogurt.
>
> D. On the bottom shelf sit plastic containers of leftovers.
>
> E. There are two drawers in the bottom of the refrigerator.

> My roommate is an organized person, and his half of our refrigerator really reflects his personality.

Practice 5: Identifying Adjectives (page 106)

Sentence 2: main, paint, black, blue, green, yellow, white, different
Sentence 3: terrible
Sentence 4: several, big
Sentence 5: broken, strong
Sentence 6: back, rusty, front, cracked
Sentence 7: terrible
Sentence 8: passenger, door, missing, passenger
Sentence 9: ten, large
Sentence 10: gas, broken
Sentence 11: (none)
Sentence 12: broken
Sentence 13: first, old, few, my, perfect
Question 2: outside to inside

Practice 6: Cumulative Adjectives (pages 108–109)

2. <u>Big</u> <u>black</u> clouds announced an approaching rainstorm.
3. <u>Colorful</u> <u>rectangular</u> flags hung from every window. (Note that *colorful* is not a color; it's an opinion.)

4. Children played on the <u>thick</u> <u>green</u> grass.
5. I dream about relaxing on a <u>beautiful</u> <u>white</u> <u>sand</u> beach.
6. They got married in a <u>small</u> <u>Italian</u> <u>stone</u> church.
7. The parents left <u>their</u> <u>two</u> <u>young</u> children with the grandparents while they worked.
8. <u>Mr. Thompson's</u> <u>advanced</u> <u>English</u> class has thirty students.
9. The real estate agent pointed out <u>several</u> <u>minor</u> problems with the house.
10. <u>Four</u> <u>large</u> <u>bedroom</u> windows were broken.

Practice 7: Coordinate Adjectives (page 110)

2. Most students like friendly, enthusiastic, imaginative teachers.
3. I am tired of the cold, rainy weather.
4. I am looking forward to the warm, sunny, relaxing days of summer.
5. The prince in a fairy tale is either tall, dark, and handsome or tall, blond, and handsome.
6. A fairy-tale prince is never short, bald, and ugly.

Practice 8: Cumulative and Coordinate Adjectives (page 110)

2. <u>Four</u> <u>shiny</u> <u>black</u> limousines were parked outside the hotel. *(cum cum cum)*

3. The <u>small</u> <u>red</u> apples looked <u>sweet</u>, <u>crisp</u>, <u>juicy</u>, and <u>delicious</u>. *(cum cum — coord coord coord coord)*

4. Hundreds of <u>happy</u>, <u>cheering</u> <u>football</u> fans ran onto the field. *(coord coord cum)*

5. The <u>pretty</u> <u>new</u> <u>French</u> teacher is from Quebec. *(cum cum cum)*

6. My father bought a <u>beautiful</u> <u>antique</u> <u>Persian</u> rug as a <u>twentieth</u> <u>anniversary</u> gift for my mother. *(cum cum cum cum cum)*

Practice 9: Editing Adjectives (page 110)

1. The hungry, frightened dog waited for someone to feed him.
2. The little black dog waited for someone to feed him.
3. My mother always bakes a delicious chocolate cake for my little brother's birthday.
4. For his tenth birthday, he received a new metal baseball bat.
5. The coach's enthusiastic, supportive manner gave the team confidence.

Practice 10: Writing Sentences with Adjectives (page 111)

Individual answers. Sample responses:
2. I also saw a pair of *dirty, smelly sports socks.*
3. Then I discovered a box of *broken yellow pencils.*
4. Next to it, I found a greasy paper bag *with dried-up french fries* inside it.
5. The discovery of *several empty soda bottles and cans* didn't surprise me.

ESL Department
Utah Valley University

Questions on the Model (page 114)

My Desk

¹The inside (of my desk) looks (like a second-hand store). ²Each drawer is full (of junk). ³(In the center drawer), you can find paper clips, erasers, pencils, pens, rubber bands, and small bottles (of glue). ⁴I have a small hardware store (in my top drawer). ⁵If you want to repair something, you can find whatever you need there. ⁶(In the second drawer), I keep snacks in case I get hungry (at night). ⁷Small items (of clothing) are (in the third drawer), and the bottom drawer holds my collection (of wind-up toys). ⁸I play (with them) (during study breaks). ⁹I have such a variety (of things) (in my desk) that I could start a small business, (according to my friends).

1. Top to bottom.
2. There are 16 prepositional phrases in the paragraph.
3. Five of them tell where something is: *in the center drawer, in my top drawer, in the second drawer, in the third drawer, in my desk.*

Practice 11: Prepositional Phrases (pages 115–116)

A.
My Favorite Place

¹My favorite place (on the campus) (of our school) is the lawn (in front of the library). ²(During my lunch break), I go there to relax (with friends). ³(In the center) (of the lawn), there is a fountain. ⁴Water splashes (from the fountain) (onto some rocks) (around it). ⁵The sound (of the splashing water) reminds me (of a place) (in the mountains) where we go (in the summer). ⁶(Under a group) (of trees) (at the edge) (of the lawn) are wooden benches and tables. ⁷(On warm days), students sit at the tables (in the shade) (of the trees) to eat their lunches. ⁸The chatter (of students) makes studying impossible. ⁹(After lunch), it becomes quiet again.

B.
My Childhood Hideout

¹I had a secret hiding place (near my childhood home). ²No one knew (of its existence), so it became my refuge (from the world). ³I often went there to escape (from my older) (brothers and sisters). ⁴I would sit alone (for hours) and daydream. ⁵I was quite comfortable (in my hideout). ⁶An old rug covered the floor. ⁷A pillow and blanket that I had permanently "borrowed" (from my oldest [and meanest] brother) were along one wall. ⁸A metal box (with a strong lid) was (in the corner). ⁹The box contained snacks, a flashlight, and a few (of my favorite mystery novels). ¹⁰I could spend all day (in my hideout).

Rewritten paragraphs will vary. Sample paragraph:

I had a secret hiding place near my childhood home. No one knew of its existence, so it became my refuge from the world. I often went there to escape from my older brothers and sisters. For hours, I would sit alone and daydream. I was quite comfortable in my hideout. An old rug covered the floor. Along one wall were a pillow and blanket that I had permanently "borrowed" from my oldest (and meanest) brother. In the corner was a metal box with a strong lid. The box contained snacks, a flashlight, and a few of my favorite mystery novels. I could spend all day in my hideout.

Try It Out! (pages 117–118)

Answers will vary. Sample paragraph:

The Shared Refrigerator (continued)

My half of our refrigerator is messy and disorganized. On the top shelf sits a box of broken eggs. Old carrots and brown salami share the second shelf with hard green bread and soft lettuce. On the third shelf, leftover pizza lies under a bowl of three-week-old spaghetti. The bottom drawer holds an interesting combination of paper bags of food from McDonald's, Taco Bell, and the Chinese Kitchen. A disgusting, smelly puddle covers the bottom. My roommate and I are different, but we get along very well.

Review Questions (page 119)

1. (1) Use space order to organize your description and (2) use lots of descriptive details.
2. Top to bottom, bottom to top, right to left, left to right, far to near, near to far, outside to inside, inside to outside.
3. Use lots of descriptive details.
4. An adjective describes a noun or pronoun.
5. (1) before nouns and (2) after linking verbs.
6. Cumulative adjectives must follow a particular order. No, you do not use commas with cumulative adjectives.
7. Coordinate adjectives do not follow a particular order. Yes, you put commas between coordinate adjectives.
8. A prepositional phrase is a preposition + a noun or noun phrase.
9. (1) Prepositional phrases of time, which answer the question "When" and (2) prepositional phrases of place, which answer the question "Where".
10. Begin some sentences with prepositional phrases of time and place.

ESL Department
Utah Valley University

21

Chapter 5: Stating Reasons and Using Examples

Questions on the Model (page 124)
1. Costa Rica.
2. The first sentence: Costa Rica is a great place to spend a vacation for two reasons. It gives the information that there are two reasons.
3. There are seven supporting sentences.
4. Two reasons. *First of all* and *Second* introduce them.
5. Two examples are given for each reason. *For example* and *For instance* introduce some of the examples.
6. The last sentence: Indeed, Costa Rica is a wonderful place to go if you love the outdoors.
7. Listing order.

Practice 1: Specific Examples (pages 126–129)
A. Answers will vary. Sample responses:
    A. 2. The grilled chicken is moist and tender.
    B. 1. Your order is ready in 3 minutes or less.
       2. The people who take your order always smile and say, "Thank you."
    C. 1. A double cheeseburger costs only $2.50.
       2. Many items are only $1.00.

B. Answers will vary. Sample responses:
    A. The pizza is tasteless.
       1. The cheese is like rubber.
       2. The crust tastes like burned cardboard.
    B. The service is slow and unprofessional.
       1. We had to wait over an hour last week for our pizza, and we were the only customers.
       2. When the server finally brought our pizza, she didn't bring us anything to eat it with.
    C. The prices are high.
       1. A medium-sized plain cheese pizza costs over $15.00.
       2. A small side salad is $5.00

C. Topic 1
    Topic Sentence: There are at least two reasons for not buying the huge, military-type vehicle called a Hummer.
    A. Hummers are big gas hogs.
       1. The H2 model gets less than 10 miles per gallon of gas.
       2. When gas costs $3 per gallon, it costs $100 to fill up a Hummer's big gas tank.

B. Hummers are bad for the environment.
  1. In one year, a Hummer gives off 24,100 pounds of carbon dioxide, which is two to three times more than average cars give off.
  2. The U.S. government's Environmental Protection Agency gives it a failing grade.
Conclusion: To sum up, for the health of your bank balance as well as for the health of the environment, don't buy a Hummer.

Topic 2
Topic Sentence: The Smart will be the next "cool" car to buy for several reasons.
  A. The design is eye-catching.
    1. It has changeable door panels in stylish colors.
    2. Its body is modern in design.
  B. The Smart is easy on the wallet.
    1. It costs between $15,000 and $25,000.
    2. The European model gets 60 miles per gallon of gas, and the U.S. model 50 miles per gallon.
  C. The Smart is easy to park.
    1. It is only 8 feet, 2-1/2 inches (250 cm) long, which is the width of a street parking space.
    2. You can park two or three Smarts side-by-side in a single street parking space.
Conclusion: For style, economy, and easy parking, the Smart is the car to buy.

Practice 2: Transition Signals with Reasons (pages 130–131)
Answers will vary. Sample responses:
Reason 4
  a. Fourth, hotels and restaurants are inexpensive.
  b. A fourth reason is that hotels and restaurants are inexpensive.

Reason 5
  a. Fifth, the people are friendly to tourists.
  b. A fifth reason is the friendliness of the people to tourists. (OR)
     A fifth reason is that the people are friendly to tourists.

Practice 3: Transition Signals with Examples (pages 132–133)
Answers will vary. Sample responses:
A. 1. Denmark has many attractions for children, such as Tivoli Gardens and Legoland.
   2. Japan is famous for its beautiful gardens. For example, the rock garden of Ryoanji Temple is known all over the world.
   3. In São Paulo, there is a mix of architecture. You can see traditional architecture in some buildings, for example, the Martinelli Building and Banco do Estado de São Paulo.
   4. There are also many modern buildings in São Paulo. For instance, the Banco Sumitomo and Conjunto Nacional are very modern in design.
   5. Bolivia offers tourists many interesting places to visit, for instance, the capital city of La Paz and the islands in Lake Titicaca.

B. Answers will vary. Sample responses:
   1. San Francisco has several ethnic neighborhoods, <u>such as</u> North Beach (Italian), the Mission District (Hispanic), and Chinatown (Chinese).
   2. When you visit the ethnic neighborhoods of Miami, you feel that you are in a foreign country. <u>For instance</u>, in Little Havana you can easily imagine that you are in Cuba.
   3. Summers are much cooler in San Francisco than in Los Angeles. <u>For example</u>, the average July temperature in San Francisco is about 65 °F, but it is 85 °F in Los Angeles.
   4. Mexico's Yucatán Peninsula has many luxury beach resorts, <u>such as</u> Cancún and Cozumel.
   5. The Yucatán is full of archaeological treasures, <u>for instance</u>, the Mayan ruins at Chichén Itzá and Tulum.

Practice 4: Complex Sentences (pages 135–136)
   A. 2. (Since) summers are hot in Arizona, <u>the best time to go there is the spring or fall.</u>
      3. (If) you are interested in Native Americans, <u>you should visit the Navajo and Hopi reservations in northern Arizona.</u>
      4. <u>You might be able to visit a tribal fair</u> (if) you are lucky.
      5. <u>The Navajo call themselves a "nation"</u> (because) they govern themselves.
      6. (Because) the Navajo language is so difficult, <u>the U.S. military used it for secret messages during World War II.</u>

   B. Answers will vary. Sample responses:
      2. I take a trip whenever <u>I have a few days' vacation.</u>
      3. After <u>I graduate,</u> I plan to work my way around the world.
      4. Before <u>I get married and start a family,</u> I want to see as much of the world as possible.
      5. I have to travel now because <u>most employers give only two weeks' vacation per year.</u>
      6. If <u>I have enough money and enough time,</u> I want to spend at least one year on the road.

Practice 5: Editing Sentence and Punctuation Errors (page 136)
       2. Since the game began in England about 150 years ago, it has spread to every corner of the globe.
 3 and 4. Millions of people go to soccer stadiums to watch their favorite team while millions more watch on television.
       6. Anyone can afford to play soccer because it doesn't require expensive equipment.
       7. Also, it has simple rules.
       8. Soccer is the number one sport in most of the world, but it is not the most popular sport in North America.
       9. Ice hockey is the favorite in Canada, and American football is the favorite in the United States.

My Love-Hate Relationship with Camping

There are two reasons I love camping and two reasons I hate camping. First of all, living outdoors for a few days refreshes my mind and renews my spirit. After I have spent a few days in nature, I feel free and happy again. Second, camping brings my family closer together because everyone helps plan the trip, set up the campsite, and prepare the meals. On the other hand, sometimes I hate camping. One reason is that I don't sleep well. I hate to sleep on the ground because the ground is hard. When I get up in the morning, I can hardly move. My back hurts, and my muscles ache. The second reason I hate camping is that we always forget something important. We forgot to bring our tent last year, so we had to sleep in the open. I didn't sleep at all because I am afraid of snakes and bugs. If I see a snake or a bug, I am frozen with fear. Why do I continue to go camping when I have such a love-hate relationship with it?

Practice 6: Capitalization Review (page 140)

September 3, 20—

Dear Miki,

Well, here I am in New York City. I still can't believe that I'm actually here! I arrived on Saturday after a long flight from Paris on Air France. The food was excellent, and so was the movie. We saw *Gone with the Wind*. I stayed Saturday and Sunday nights at the Fairmount Hotel near Rockefeller Center. Then on Monday I moved into my dormitory at NYU.

I spent my entire first weekend here sightseeing. I saw many famous places: Rockefeller Center, the United Nations, the Guggenheim Museum, the NY Stock Exchange, and the Statue of Liberty. I window-shopped at Gucci and Saks Fifth Avenue. I also visited another famous art museum and the NBC television studios.

Today is a holiday in the United States. It is Labor Day, so all of the government offices, schools, and banks are closed. People in the United States celebrate the end of summer by having a three-day weekend. Many New Yorkers spend the day in Central Park or go to the beach on Long Island.

I learned some interesting things about New York. Its nickname is "The Big Apple," but no one knows why it's called an apple and not a banana or an orange. Another interesting fact is that the first Europeans who came here bought Manhattan Island from the natives for only $24.00. Of course, it's now worth trillions of dollars.

Well, that's all for now. Classes begin next week. I'm having a good time, but I miss you all, and I really miss French food. Write soon.

With love,
Nicole

Practice 7: Commas (pages 142–143)

A.   1. (No commas required.)

2. For example, one of my classmates takes six units and works forty hours a week.

3. Since he is also married and has two children, he is a very busy person.

4. He works at night, attends class in the morning, and sleeps when he can.

5. When he fell asleep in class yesterday, we decided not to wake him up.

6. Scientists believe that animals can think, feel, and communicate just as humans can.

7. (No commas required.)

8. For instance, when he does something bad, he looks guilty.

9. He hangs his head, drops his tail, and looks up at me with sad eyes.

10. Later, we usually discover the reason for his guilty looks, but it's hard to punish him.

11. China is the country with the largest population, but with a land area of 17,075,400 square kilometers, Russia is the largest country in size.

12. My mother lives in Miami, Florida in the winter and in Denver, Colorado in the summer.

13. When it becomes too hot in Florida, she moves to Colorado.

14. (No commas required.)

15. Her address in Florida is P.O. Box 695, Miami, Florida 33167, and her address in Colorado is 3562 State Street, Apt. 3-C, Denver, Colorado 80210.

16. On Sunday, June 10, 2007, I graduated from college.

17. Then on Monday, June 11, 2007, I started looking for a job.

B. Individual responses.

Review Questions (pages 143–144)

1. Listing order.

2. *For instance, for example, such as.*

3. *For instance* and *For example.*

4. You can use all three.

5. *Because* and *since.*

6. *If.*

7. Put a comma after an dependent clause when the dependent clause comes before an independent clause.

8. See page 139 in the text.

    See page 141 in the text.

Chapter 6: Expressing Your Opinion

Questions on the Model (page 150)

1. The writer's opinion is that violent video games are harmful to young people. She uses the phrase "In my opinion."
2. Three reasons.
3. Listing order.
4. Answers may vary, but students might choose the last reason as the strongest because it is supported by a shocking example.

Practice 1: Analyzing an Opinion Paragraph (page 151)

Video Games and Violence

Topic Sentence	In my opinion, violent video games are harmful to young people.	(Opinion)
First Reason	A. Playing these games can cause changes in the behavior of young people.	(Opinion)
Detail	1. According to psychologists, frequent players have poorer grades in school.	(Fact)
Detail	2. They are also more hostile and act more aggressively toward their teachers and classmates.	(Fact)
Second Reason	B. They make young people less sensitive to violence in the real world.	(Opinion)
Detail	1. The games make it fun to shoot and kill, and the line between play violence and real violence becomes very thin or disappears entirely.	(Opinion)
Detail	2. Noah Wilson was stabbed to death by a friend who often played the violent game "Mortal Combat."	(Fact)
Detail	3. Noah's mother said, "The boy who stabbed him was acting out the part of Cyrex."	(Fact)
Third Reason	C. They teach players to use violence to solve problems.	(Opinion)
Detail	1. If classmates tease you, don't try to work it out—bring a gun to school and shoot them.	(Opinion)
Detail	2. Story of the Columbine High School massacre.	(Fact)
Detail	3. The two killers were fans of the games "Doom" and "Wolfenstein 3D."	(Fact)
Concluding Sentence	For these three reasons, I feel that violent video games are harmful to young people and should be controlled—or, even better, banned.	

ESL Department
Utah Valley University

Practice 2:   Outlining an Opinion Paragraph (pages 153–155)

2. Answers may vary. Sample responses:

Capital Punishment

Topic Sentence	In my opinion, capital punishment is wrong.
First Reason	A. It is wrong to kill another human.
Possible Details	Only God has the right to take a life. Quotes from religions? Buddhist teachings? Christian Bible?
Second Reason	B. It does not deter crime.
Possible Details	Statistics on crime in places that have capital punishment compared to places that don't have it?
Third Reason	C. Sometimes people who have been sentenced to death are later found to be innocent.
Possible Details	Statistics?
Concluding Sentence	For these three reasons, I believe that capital punishment should be abolished in the places where it exists.

3. Answers may vary. Sample responses:

Using Cell Phones in Public Places

Topic Sentence	In my opinion, people who use cell phones in public should be fined for extreme rudeness.
First Reason	A. In movie theaters, concerts, and at sporting events, you have paid a lot of money to watch a movie or hear a concert, not to listen to someone talking on his or her cell phone.
Possible Details	Poll of classmates on how often they have been disturbed by cell phone conversations at these places. Get quotations about their reactions.
Second Reason	B. In some places, you are trapped into listening to someone's private conversations; you cannot escape.
Possible Details	Crowded buses or subways, elevators, restaurants, waiting in line. Survey classmates on how often this has happened to them and their reactions.
Third Reason	C. Using a cell phone while driving is dangerous.
Possible Details	Statistics on accidents caused by drivers talking on their cell phones. (Internet or library)
Concluding Sentence	In conclusion, cell phones are popular and useful, but people should not have the freedom to use them whenever and wherever they want to.

4. Individual responses.

Questions on the Model (page 157)
1. Three reasons.
2. The first 2 reasons are supported with facts. The last reason is not.

Practice 3: Adjective Clauses with *who, which,* and *that* (pages 158–159)

A. 2. His mother, (who) neglected him and his brothers, wants to keep him.
   3. He wants to be adopted by the Russes, (who) are his foster parents.
   4. Foster parents are people (who) take care of abused or neglected children.
   5. A box (that) contained marijuana was in the living room.
   6. Mrs. Kingsley smoked marijuana, (which) is an illegal drug.
   7. The boys' father, (who) did not live with their mother, did not want the children to live with him.
   8. This case, (which) was the first child-parent divorce in the United States, received a lot of attention.
   9. The lawyer (who) represented Mrs. Kingsley was a woman.
   10. The judge made a decision (that) most people agree with.

B. 2. Sometimes the parents, who (know) their child better than anyone, choose. (plural)
   3. Sometimes the parents hire a matchmaker, who (charges) a fee to find a suitable person. (singular)
   4. The two young people are probably very nervous at their first meeting, which usually (takes place) in the bride's home. (singular)
   5. In some cultures, a young man or woman who (doesn't like) the parents' or matchmaker's choice may say "no." (singular)
   6. Marrying for love, which (is) the custom in most Western cultures, does not guarantee happiness. (singular)
   7. The divorce rate among couples who (marry) for love is very high. (plural)
   8. People who (listened) only to their hearts sometimes wish they had listened to their heads. (plural)

Practice 4: Punctuating Adjective Clauses (page 161)

A. 3. A pediatrician is a doctor who <u>takes care of children</u>.
   4. Dr. Jones, who <u>is our neighbor</u>, is a pediatrician.
   5. Students who <u>studied</u> got A's on the final exam.
   6. Gabriela and Trinh, who <u>studied</u>, got A's on the final exam.
   7. My birthday is next Monday, which <u>is a holiday</u>.
   8. A holiday that <u>is especially fun for children</u> is Halloween.

29

B.   **The Story of Coca-Cola**

[1]A popular beverage that is sold all over the world is Coca-Cola. [2]A doctor who lived in Atlanta, Georgia invented it in 1886. [3]Dr. John Pemberton, who was also a pharmacist, first sold Coca-Cola as a nerve tonic, stimulant, and headache medicine. [4]The name of the dark brown syrup that made people feel better was "Pemberton's French Wine Coca." [5]Later, someone added soda water to the syrup, and it became the beverage that is our modern Coca-Cola. [6]The first part of the name (*coca*) comes from *cocaine*, which was one of the original ingredients. [7]The second part of the name (*cola*) comes from *kola nut*, which is still an ingredient. [8]The original formula has changed over the years. [9]Of course, Coca-Cola no longer contains cocaine, which is an illegal drug, but it still tastes delicious. [10]The formula for Coca-Cola is a secret that is carefully guarded.

Practice 5: Sentences with Adjective Clauses (pages 162–166)
Answers will vary.

A. 2. The purse that (or which) is lying under the chair is hers.
    3. Alice, who is my best friend, moved to New York last month.
    4. She is living in an apartment that (or which) has a view of Central Park.
    5. On our honeymoon, we stayed at the Bellagio, which is our favorite hotel in Las Vegas.
    6. Uncle John, who owns a house on every continent, his own private jet, and two yachts, has everything.
    7. A person who has love has everything.

B.   who (people)
    3. Mr. and Mrs. Haddad are very traditional. ~~Mr. and Mrs. Haddad~~ are from Lebanon.
       Mr. and Mrs. Haddad, who are from Lebanon, are very traditional.

                                                         who (people)
    4. Jamila is the oldest daughter in the Haddad family. ~~The Haddad family~~ immigrated to this country seven years ago.
       Jamila is the oldest daughter in the Haddad family, who immigrated to this country seven years ago.

                                                    who (person)
    5. Her parents want her to marry a man. ~~The man~~ is thirty-two years old.
       Her parents want her to marry a man who is thirty-two years old.

                                                  which (thing)
    6. The husband-to-be lives in Lebanon. ~~Lebanon~~ is a country in the Middle East.
       The husband-to-be lives in Lebanon, which is a country in the Middle East.

                                              that/which (thing)
    7. He owns a business. ~~The business~~ is very successful.
       He owns a business that (*or* which) is very successful.

                                             who (people)
    8. People say that he is very nice. ~~People~~ know him.
       People who know him say that he is very nice.

30

who (person)

9. Jamila ran away from home rather than marry the man. ~~She~~ wants to go to college in her new country.
   Jamila, who wants to go to college in her new country, ran away from home rather than marry the man.

who (people)

10. Mr. and Mrs. Haddad don't understand why she ran away. ~~Mr. and Mrs. Haddad~~ thought they had arranged a good future for their daughter.
    Mr. and Mrs. Haddad, who thought they had arranged a good future for their daughter, don't understand why she ran away.

C. 2. Carrots are vegetables which are orange in color.
   3. A vegetarian is a person who doesn't eat meat.
   4. A hybrid is an automobile which runs on electricity and gasoline.
   5. Orphans are children who have no parents.
   6. A giant panda is an animal that lives in China.
   7. An ichthyologist is a scientist who studies fish.

Answers will vary for items 9–12. Possible definitions:
   9. A cow is an animal that (or which) gives milk.
   10. A jockey is a person who rides horses in races.
   11. A dental hygienist is a person who cleans teeth.
   12. An eel is a fish that (or which) looks like a snake.

D. Answers will vary. Possible sentences:
   2. A kilt, which looks like a skirt, is traditional men's clothing from Scotland.
   3. Warmack became interested in his Scottish heritage after seeing the movie *Braveheart*, which is about Scottish history.
   4. The vice-principal, who joked with him about the kilt, didn't tell him not to wear it.
   5. Rick McClard, who is the principal of the school, told him to change into a pair of pants.
   6. Scottish heritage organizations, which support Warmack, are collecting items of clothing to complete his outfit.

Practice 6: Fragments (page 168)
   Sentences 1, 3, 5, 7, and 10 are fragments.
   Corrections will vary. Suggested corrections:
   3. For example, more women work in the field of medicine.
   5. Medical schools, which didn't use to accept many women, now have many women students.
   7. Men are also working in traditional female occupations, such as nursing, which used to be a woman's profession.
   10. Her dream is to supervise the construction of bridges and dams.

Practice 7: Editing Fragments (pages 168–169)

Sentences 3, 7, 12, 13, and 15 are fragments.

Corrections will vary. Suggested corrections:

7. Many religions have special clothing and symbols, such as turbans, headscarves, and crosses.
12. It is their right to follow their beliefs.
13. It is wrong for a school to take away that right.
15. If a school bans only head coverings, this is discrimination.

Practice 8: Punctuating Quotations (pages 170–171)

2. "Why not?" I asked.
3. "Medical care in the United States is too expensive," they answered.
4. According to a little book about healthcare in the United States, a two-hour visit to the emergency room can cost more than $3,000.
5. I asked, "What happens if I can't pay?"
6. "I don't know," my father replied, "but I think you should find out."
7. According to the booklet, "The school will provide medical insurance while you are a student."
8. My advisor said, "It doesn't cover everything, so you might want to buy additional insurance from a private company."

Review Questions (page 171)

1. A fact is a true statement that no one can disagree with. An opinion is a statement of someone's belief.
2. Yes.
3. Facts are stronger support.
4. It is called an adjective clause because it acts like an adjective; that is, it gives more information about a noun or pronoun.
5. *Who.*
6. *Which, that.*
7. Use commas around an adjective clause that gives extra information about the noun it modifies.
8. No.
9. The independent clause is incomplete. To fix it, complete the independent clause; <u>Students</u> who fail the same class three times <u>cannot take it again</u>.
10. See the rules on page 170.
11. *He says, according to.*